MYSTICAL POWER

PSALMS

Nathaniel J. Harris

ISBN 978-1-291-583120

Introduction

These are the prayers of David, father of Solomon king of Israel, over which no sorcery holds sway. Trust in the LORD, God before all gods, who shall endure beyond the end of the earth. *Amen.*

Wise men throughout the generations have recognized the mystical power of the Psalms to get *results*; from attracting love and wealth, to overcoming adversaries, and banishing the powers of evil. Their efficacious employment in all manner of magical spells is well recorded.

Traditionally, Psalms have been copied on to virgin parchment in red ink, sealed into 'charm bags' along with empowering items such as mandrake or high john conquerer roots, and never allowed to touch the ground. Sometimes, the parchment is eaten as a consecrated 'host'. Practitioners of candle magic recite them during rituals, often 'dressing' the candles with sacred oils, and burning different colours for various purposes. Along with other prayers, the

Psalms make regular appearance in the pages of the classical grimoires, such as the famed *Key of Solomon,* wherein instruction is given for the summoning and binding of demons. It would be easy to fill a book with thousands of such rituals.

Yet these are not mere incantations, to be repeated with an empty heart. God will not grant petty wishes for the insincere. He will not be directed by the will of liars, nor serve the pride of the boastful.

Pay heed to these words, and follow their advice closely. Instruction is given towards meditation; seeking wisdom of the soul. It will do you no good merely to recite *Psalm 109* in expectation of destroying one's enemies; one must also fast, and humble oneself, or the words spoken will not be true. *Psalm 18* will protect your home, yet not if the door is left unlocked at night, or if the untrustworthy are allowed admittance. Nor will the recitation of *Psalm 92* bring promotion to the lazy and undeserving, or *Psalm 5* give protection to the guilty. Yet to those who trust in the LORD, and who faithfully hold his precepts, great favours shall be granted.

Foolish men have said the laws of God do not apply to them, because they do not believe. They have assumed their atheism allows them to act immorally. Yet all choices in life, regardless of faith, have consequences. Vain men, easily distracted by immature pleasures, shall surely suffer accordingly; for they are veered by every circumstance, and lose control of their own destiny. The upright and modest man, who acts with wisdom, shall not suffer thus; they shall dwell safely, and be quiet from fear of evil. This remains so whether one recognizes the LORD as ultimate truth, as a spiritual symbol for what may not be understood by intellect, or whether one denies him entirely; his laws apply equally, for they are the very laws of nature.

There are many who mistakenly believe the rational sciences have disproven God, and that we have outgrown the superstitions of religion. Whilst lesser minds, such as Dwarkins, may tend towards atheism, many of the greatest, including Einstein and Plank, have reasoned a vaster consciousness is behind the evolution of the cosmos. The myth of Genesis may be interpreted as symbolic, yet science has not 'killed God'; rather, it has increased our sense of wonder at the immensity of all creation.

In this age we like to speak of objective (outer) and subjective (inner) reality, as if the two are separate phenomena. Whilst it is easy to comprehend how events in the objective world may effect our subjective reality, it is often much harder to understand how our subjective attitude may effect our experiences in the objective world. Yet what we believe dictates our actions, perceptions, and interpretation of phenomena. Hence it is that the faithless do not know the LORD, yet to those with eyes to see, he is all around. As wise men have said, 'If you cannot find God within yourself, you shall never find him without'.

Most foolish is the belief that any one church may have monopoly on the knowledge of God. That men should make war in the name of religion is the greatest absurdity and the greatest tragedy; yet more blood has been shed in this cause than any other. Remember, then, that the Bible is a book *about* God; yet it is not God *himself*. Whatever the origins of the words, they have been interpreted, translated, and even edited, by mortal men. As it says in *Psalm 133*, 'Behold, how good and how pleasant *it is* for brethren to dwell together in unity!'

God is Love,
Nathaniel J. Harris

Psalm 1

To aid in settling a disturbed home, and to diminish the power of enemies.

Blessed *is* the man that walketh not in the counsel of the ungodly, nor standeth in the way of sinners, nor sitteth in the seat of the scornful.

2 But his delight *is* in the law of the LORD; and in his law doth he meditate day and night.

3 And he shall be like a tree planted by the rivers of water, that bringeth forth his fruit in his season; his leaf also shall not wither; and whatsoever he doeth shall prosper.

4 The ungodly *are* not so: but *are* like the chaff which the wind driveth away.

5 Therefore the ungodly shall not stand in the judgment, nor sinners in the congregation of the righteous.

6 For the LORD knoweth the way of the righteous: but the way of the ungodly shall perish.

Psalm 2

To prevent slander. In extreme situations, to bring about the death of an enemy.

Why do the heathen rage, and the people imagine a vain thing?

2 The kings of the earth set themselves, and the rulers take counsel together, against the LORD, and against his anointed, *saying,*

3 Let us break their bands asunder, and cast away their cords from us.

4 He that sitteth in the heavens shall laugh: the Lord shall have them in derision.

5 Then shall he speak unto them in his wrath, and vex them in his sore displeasure.

6 Yet have I set my king upon my holy hill of Zion.

7 I will declare the decree: the LORD hath said unto me, Thou *art* my Son; this day have I begotten thee.

8 Ask of me, and I shall give *thee* the heathen *for* thine inheritance, and the uttermost parts of the earth *for* thy possession.

9 Thou shalt break them with a rod of iron; thou shalt dash them in pieces like a potter's vessel.

10 Be wise now therefore, O ye kings: be instructed, ye judges of the earth.

3

11 Serve the LORD with fear, and rejoice with trembling.

12 Kiss the Son, lest he be angry, and ye perish *from* the way, when his wrath is kindled but a little. Blessed *are* all they that put their trust in him.

Psalm 3

To overcome fear. To break up a love affair.

A Psalm of David, when he fled from Absalom his son.

LORD, how are they increased that trouble me! Many *are* they that rise up against me.

2 Many *there be* which say of my soul, *There is* no help for him in God. Selah.

3 But thou, O LORD, *art* a shield for me; my glory, and the lifter of mine head.

4 I cried unto the LORD with my voice, and he heard me out of his holy hill. Selah.

5 I laid me down and slept; I awaked; for the LORD sustained me.

6 I will not be afraid of ten thousands of people, that have set *themselves* against me round about.

7 Arise, O LORD; save me, O my God: for thou hast smitten all mine enemies *upon* the cheek bone; thou hast broken the teeth of the ungodly.

8 Salvation *belongeth* unto the LORD: thy blessing *is* upon the people. Selah.

Psalm 5

To win a lawsuit.

To the chief Musician upon Nehiloth, A Psalm of David.

Give ear to my words, O LORD, consider my meditation.

2 Hearken unto the voice of my cry, my King, and my God: for unto thee will I pray.

3 My voice shalt thou hear in the morning, O LORD; in the morning will I direct *my prayer* unto thee, and will look up.

4 For thou art not a God that hath pleasure in wickedness: nor shall evil dwell with thee.

5 The foolish shall not stand in thy sight: thou hatest all the workers of iniquity.

6 Thou shall destroy them that speak leasing: the LORD abhor the bloody and deceitful man.

7 But as for me, I will come *into* thy house in the multitude of thy mercy: *and* in thy fear will I worship toward thy holy temple.

8 Lead me, O LORD, in thy righteousness because of mine enemies; make thy way straight before my face.

9 For *there* is no faithfulness in their mouth; their inward part *is* very wickedness; their throat *is* an open sepulchre; they flatter with their tongue.

10 Destroy thou them, O God; let them fall by their own counsels; cast them out in the multitude of their transgressions; for they have rebelled against thee.

11 But let all those that put their trust in thee rejoice: let them ever shout for joy, because thou defendest them: let them also that love thy name be joyful in thee.

12 For thou, LORD, wilt bless the righteous; with favour wilt thou compass him as *with* a shield.

Psalm 7

To overcome curses and bad luck.

Shiggaion of David, which he sang unto the LORD, concerning the words of Cush the Benjamite.

O LORD my God, in thee do I put my trust: save me from all them that persecute me, and deliver me:

2 Lest he tear my soul like a lion, rending *it* in pieces, while *there* is none to deliver.

3 O LORD my God, if I have done this; if there be iniquity in my hands;

4 If I have rewarded evil unto him that was at peace with me; (yea, I have delivered him that without cause is mine enemy:)

5 Let the enemy persecute my soul, and take *it*; yea, let him tread down my life upon the earth, and lay mine honour in the dust. Selah.

6 Arise, O LORD, in thin anger, lift up thyself because of the rage of mine enemies: and awake for me *to* the judgment *that* thou hast commanded.

7 So shall the congregation of the people compass thee about: for their sakes therefore return thou on high.

8 The LORD shall judge the people: judge me, O LORD, according to my righteousness, and according to mine integrity *that is* in me.

9 Oh let the wickedness of the wicked come to an end; but establish the just: for the righteous God trieth the heart and reins.

10 My defence *is* of God, which saveth the upright in heart.

11 God judgeth the righteous, and God is angry *with the wicked* every day.

12 If he turn not, he will whet his sword; he hath bent his bow and made it ready.

13 He hath also prepared for him the instruments of death; he ordaineth his arrows against the persecutors.

14 Behold, he travaileth with iniquity, and hath conceived mischief, and brought forth falsehood.

15 He made a pit, and digged it, and is fallen into the ditch *which* he made.

16 His mischief shall return upon his own head, and his violent dealing shall come down upon his own pate.

17 I will praise the LORD according to his righteousness: and will sing praise to the name of the LORD most high.

Psalm 8

To gain employment, attract custom, and do well in business.

To the Musician upon Gittith, A Psalm of David.

O LORD our Lord, how excellent is thy name in all the earth! Who hast set thy glory above the heavens.

2 Out of the mouths of babes and sucklings hast thou ordained strength because of thine enemies, that thou mightest still the enemy and the avenger.

3 When I consider thy heavens, the work of thy fingers, the moon and the stars, which thou hast ordained;

4 What is man, that thou art mindful of him? And the son of man, that thou visitest him?

5 For thou hast made him a little lower than thine angels, and has crowned him with glory and honour.

6 Thou madest him to have dominion over the works of thy hands; thou hast put all *things* under his feet.

7 All sheep and oxen, yea, and the beasts of the field;

8 The fowl of the air, and the fish of the sea, *and whatsoever* passeth through the paths of the seas.

9 O LORD our Lord, how excellent *is* thy name in all the earth!

Psalm 9

To overcome enemies.

To the chief Musician upon Muthlabben, A Psalm of David.

I will praise thee, O LORD, with my whole heart; I will shew forth all thy marvelous works.

2 I will be glad and rejoice in thee: I will sing praise to thy name, O thou most High.

3 When mine enemies are turned back, they shall fall and perish at thy presence.

4 For thou hast maintained my right and my cause; thou satest in the throne judging right.

5 Thou hast rebuked the heathen, thou hast destroyed the wicked, thou hast put out their name for ever and ever.

6 O thou enemy, destructions are come to a perpetual end: and thou hast destroyed cities; their memorial is perished with them.

7 But the LORD shall endure for ever: he hath prepared his throne for judgement.

8 And he shall judge the world in righteousness, he shall minister judgement to the people in uprightness.

9 The LORD also will be a refuge for the oppressed, a refuge in times of trouble.

10 And they that know thy name will put their trust in thee: for thou, LORD, hast not forsaken them that seek thee.

11 Sing praises to the LORD, which dwelleth in Zion: declare amongst the people his doings.

12 When he maketh inquisition for blood, he remebereth them: he forgetteth not the cry of the humble.

13 Have mercy upon me, O LORD; consider my trouble which I suffer of them that hate me, thou that liftest me up from the gates of death:

14 That I may shew forth all thy praise in the gates of the daughter of Zion: I will rejoice in thy salvation.

15 The heathen are sunk down in the pit *that* they made: in the net which they hid is their own foot taken.

16 The LORD is known *by* the judgment *which* he executeth: the wicked is snared in the work of his own hands. Higgaion. Selah.

17 The wicked shall be turned into hell, *and* all the nations that forget God.

18 For the needy shall not always be forgotten: the expectation of the poor shall *not* perish for ever.

19 Arise, O LORD; let not man prevail: let the heathen be judged in thy sight.

20 Put them in fear, O LORD: *that* the nations may know themselves *to be but* men. Selah.

Psalm 10

To strengthen willpower. To prevail against the odds.

Why standeth thou afar off, O LORD? *Why* hidest thou *thyself* in times of trouble?

2 The wicked in *his* pride doth persecute the poor: let them be taken in the devices that they have imagined.

3 For the wicked boasteth of his heart's desire, and blesseth the covetous, *whom* the LORD abhorreth.

4 The wicked, through the pride of his countenance, will not seek *after God*: God *is* not in all his thoughts.

5 His ways are always grievous; thy judgments *are* far out of his sight: *as for* all his enemies, he puffeth at them.

6 He hath said in his heart, I shall not be moved: for *I shall* never *be* in adversity.

7 His mouth is full of cursing and deceit and fraud: under his tongue *is* mischief and vanity.

8 He sitteth in the lurking places of the villages: in the secret places doth he murder the innocent: his eyes are privily set against the poor.

9 He lieth in wait secretly as a lion in his den: he lieth in wait to catch the poor: he doth catch the poor, when he draweth them into his net.

10 He croucheth, *and* humbleth himself, that the poor may fall by his strong ones.

11 He hath said in his heart, God hath forgotten: he hideth his face; he will never see *it.*

12 Arise, O LORD; O God, lift up thin hand: forget not the humble.

13 Wherefore doth the wicked contemn God? He hath said in his heart, Thou wilt not require *it.*

14 Thou hast seen *it*; for thou beholdest mischief and spite, to require *it* with thy hand: the poor committeth himself unto thee, thou art the helper of the fatherless.

15 Break thou the arm of the wicked and the evil *man*: seek out his wickedness *till* thou find none.

16 The LORD *is* King for ever and ever: the heathen are perished out of his land.

17 LORD, thou hast heard the desire of the humble: thou wilt prepare their heart, thou wilt cause thine ear to hear:

18 To judge the fatherless and the oppressed, that the man of the earth may no more oppress.

Psalm 11

To gain and maintain happiness.

To the chief Musician, A Psalm of David.

In the LORD put I my trust: how say ye to my soul, Flee *as* a bird to your mountain?

2 For, lo, the wicked bend *their* bow, they make ready their arrow upon the string, that they may privily shoot at the upright in heart.

3 If the foundations be destroyed, what can the righteous do?

4 The LORD *is* in his holy temple, the LORD's throne *is* in heaven: his eyes behold, his eyelids try, the children of men.

5 The LORD trieth the righteous: but the wicked and him that loveth violence his soul hateth.

6 Upon the wicked he shall rain snares, fire, and brimstone, and an horrible tempest: *this shall be* the portion of their cup.

7 For the righteous LORD loveth righteousness; his countenance doth behold the upright.

Psalm 12

To overcome slanderers and gossip.

To the chief Musician upon Sheminith, A Psalm of David.

Help, LORD; for the godly man ceaseth; for the faithful fail from among the children of men.

2 They speak vanity every one with his neighbour: *with* flattering lips *and* with a double heart do they speak.

3 The LORD shall cut off all flattering lips, *and* the tongue that speaketh proud things:

4 Who have said, With our tongue will we prevail: our lips are our own: who *is* the lord over us?

5 For the oppression of the poor, for the sighing of the needy, now will I arise, saith the LORD; I will set *him* in safety *from him that* puffeth at him.

6 The words of the LORD are pure words: *as* silver tried in a furnace of the earth, purified seven times.

7 Thou shalt keep them, O LORD, thou shalt preserve them from this generation for ever.

8 The wicked walk on every side, when the vilest men are exalted.

Psalm 13

To overcome depression. To protect against untimely death.

To the chief Musician, A Psalm of David.

How long wilt thou forget me, O LORD? For ever? How long wilt thou hide thy face from me?

2 How long shall I take counsel in my soul, *having* sorrow in my heart daily? How long shall my enemy be exalted over me?

3 Consider *and* hear me, O LORD my God: lighten mine eyes, lest I sleep the sleep of death;

4 Lest mine enemy say, I have prevailed against him; *and* those that troubled me rejoice when I am moved.

5 But I have trusted in thy mercy; my heart shall rejoice in thy salvation.

6 I will sing unto the LORD, because he hath dealt bountifully with me.

Psalm 14

To overcome bad luck.

To the chief Musician, A Psalm of David.

The fool hath said in his heart, *There is* no God. They are corrupt, they have done abominable works, *there is* none that doeth good.

2 The LORD looked down from heaven upon the children of men, to see if there were any that did understand, *and* seek God.

3 They are all gone aside, they are *all* together become filthy: *there is* none that doeth good, no, not one.

4 Have all the workers of iniquity no knowledge? Who eat up my people *as* they eat bread, and call not upon the LORD.

5 There were they in great fear: for God *is* in the generation of the righteous.

6 Ye have shamed the counsel of the poor, because the LORD *is* his refuge.

7 Oh that the salvation of Israel *were come* out of Zion! When the LORD bringeth back the captivity of his people, Jacob shall rejoice, *and* Israel shall be glad.

Psalm 15

Exorcism, and protection against evil spirits.

A Psalm of David.

Lord, who shall abide in thy tabernacle? Who shall dwell in thy holy hill?

2 He that walketh uprightly, and worketh righteousness, and speaketh the truth of his heart.

3 *He that* backbiteth not with his tongue, nor doeth evil to his neighbour, nor taketh up reproach against his neighbour.

4 In whose eyes a vile person is contemned; he that honoureth them that fear the LORD. *He that* sweareth to *his own* hurt, and changeth not.

5 He that putteth not out his money to usury, nor taketh reward against the innocent. He that doeth these *things* shall never be moved.

Psalm 17

To redirect one's foes away from wickedness.

A Prayer of David.

Hear the right, O LORD, attend unto my cry, give ear unto my prayer, that goeth not out of feigned lips.

2 Let my sentence come forth from thy presence; let thine eyes behold the things that are equal.

3 Thou hast proved mine heart; thou hast visited *me* in the night; thou hast tried me, *and* shalt find nothing; I am purposed *that* my mouth shall not transgress.

4 Concerning the works of men, by the word of thy lips I have kept *me from* the paths of the destroyer.

5 Hold up my goings in thy paths, *that* my footsteps slip not.

6 I have called upon thee, for thou wilt hear me, O God: incline thine ear unto me, *and hear* my speech.

7 Shew thy marvelous lovingkindness, O thou that savest by thy right hand them which put their trust *in thee* from those that rise up *against them.*

8 Keep me as the apple of the eye, hide me under the shadow of thy wings.

9 From the wicked that oppress me, *from* my deadly enemies, *who* compass me about.

10 They are inclosed in their own fat: with their mouth they speak proudly.

11 They have now compassed us in our steps: they have set their eyes bowing down to the earth.

12 Like as a lion *that* is greedy of his prey, and as it were a young lion lurking in secret places.

13 Arise, O LORD, disappoint him, cast him down: deliver my soul from the wicked, *which* is thy sword:

14 From men *which are* thy hand, O LORD, from men of the world, *which have* their portion in *this* life, and whose belly thou fillest with thy hid treasure: they are full of children, and leave the rest of their substance to their babes.

15 As for me, I will behold thy face in righteousness: I shall be satisfied, when I awake, with thy likeness.

Psalm 18

To protect the home.

To the chief Musician, A Psalm of David, the servant of the LORD, who spake unto the LORD the words of this song in the day that the LORD delivered him from the hand of all his enemies, and from the hand of Saul: and he said,

I will love thee, O LORD, my strength.

2 The LORD is my rock, and my fortress, and my deliverer; my God, my strength, in whom I will trust; my buckler, and the horn of my salvation, *and* my high tower.

3 I will call upon the LORD, *who is worthy* to be praised: so shall I be saved from mine enemies.

4 The sorrows of death compassed me, and the floods of ungodly men made me afraid.

5 The sorrows of hell compassed me about: the snares of death prevented me.

6 In my distress I called upon the LORD, and cried unto my God: he heard my voice out of his temple, and my cry came before him, *even* into his ears.

7 Then the earth shook and trembled; the foundations also of the hills moved and were shaken, because he was wroth.

8 They went up in smoke out of his nostrils, and fire out of his mouth devoured: coals were kindled by it.

9 He bowed the heavens also, and came down: and darkness *was* under his feet.

10 And he rode upon a cherub, and did fly: yea, he did fly upon the wings of the wind.

11 He made darkness his secret place; his pavilion round about him *were* dark waters *and* thick clouds of the skies.

12 At the brightness *that was* before him his thick clouds passed, hail stones and coals of fire.

13 The LORD also thundered in the heavens, and the Highest gave his voice; hail *stones* and coals of fire.

14 Yea, he sent out arrows, and scattered them; and he shot out lightenings, and discomfited them.

15 Then the channels of water were seen, and the foundations of the world were discovered at thy rebuke, O LORD, at the blast of the breath of thy nostrils.

16 He sent from above, he took me, he drew me out of many waters.

17 He delivered me from my strong enemy, and from them which hated me: for they were too strong for me.

18 They prevented me in the day of my calamity: but the LORD was my stay.

19 He brought me forth also into a large place; he delivered me, because he delighted in me.

20 The LORD rewarded me according to my righteousness; according to the cleanness of my hands he recompensed me.

21 For I have kept the ways of the LORD, and have not wickedly departed from my God.

22 For all his judgments *were* before me, and I did not put away his statutes from me.

23 I was also upright before him, and I kept myself from mine iniquity.

24 Therefore hath the LORD recompensed me according to my righteousness, according to the cleanness of my hands in his eyesight.

25 With the merciful thou wilt shew thyself merciful; with the upright man thou wilt shew thyself upright;

26 With the pure thou wilt shew thyself pure; and with the froward he will show himself froward.

27 For thou wilt save the afflicted people; but will bring down high looks.

28 For thou wilt light my candle: the LORD my God will enlighten my darkness.

29 For by thee have I run through a troop; and by my God have I leaped over a wall.

30 *As for* God, his way *is* perfect: the word of the LORD is tried: he *is* a buckler to all those who trust him.

31 For who *is* God save the LORD? Or who *is* a rock save our God?

32 *It is* God that girdeth me with strength, and maketh my way perfect.

33 He maketh my feet like hinds' *feet*, and setteth me upon high places.

34 He teacheth my hands to war, so that a bow of steel is broken by mine arms.

35 Thou hast also given me the shield of thy salvation: and thy right hand hath holden me up, and thy gentleness hath made me great.

36 Thou hast enlarged my steps under me, and my feet did not slip.

37 I have pursued mine enemies, and overtaken them: neither did I turn again till they were consumed.

38 I have wounded them that they were not able to rise: they are fallen under my feet.

39 For thou hast girded me with strength unto the battle: thou hast subdued under me those that rode up against me.

40 Thou hast also given me the necks of mine enemies; that I might destroy them that hate me.

41 They cried, but *there was* none to save *them: even* unto the LORD, but he answered them not.

42 Then did I beat them small as the dust before the wind: I did cast them out as the dirt in the streets.

43 Thou hast delivered me from the strivings of the people; *and* thou hast made me the head of the heathen: a people *whom* I have not known shall serve me.

44 As soon as they hear of me, they shall obey me: the strangers shall submit themselves unto me.

45 The strangers shall fade away, and be afraid out of their close places.

46 The LORD liveth; and blessed *be* my rock; and let the God of my salvation be exalted.

47 It is God that avengeth me, and subdueth the people under me.

48 He delivereth me from mine enemies: yea, thou liftest me up above those that rise up against me: thou hast delivered me from the violent man.

49 Therefore will I give thanks unto thee, O LORD, among the heathen, and sing praises unto thy name.

50 Great deliverance giveth he to his king; and sheweth mercy to his anointed, to David, and to his seed for ever more.

Psalm 19

A meditation.

To the chief Musician, A Psalm of David.

The heavens declare the glory of God; and the firmament sheweth his handywork.

2 Day unto day uttereth speech, and night unto night sheweth knowledge.

3 *There is* no speech nor language, where their voice is not heard.

4 Their line is gone out through all the earth, and their words to the end of the world. In them hath he set a tabernacle for the sun,

5 Which *is* as a bridegroom coming out of his chamber, and rejoiceth as a strong man to run a race.

6 His going forth is from the end of heaven, and his circuit unto the ends of it: and there is nothing hid from the heat thereof.

7 The law of the LORD *is* perfect, converting the soul: the testimony of the LORD *is* sure, making wise the simple.

8 The statutes of the LORD *are* right, rejoicing the heart: the commandment of the LORD *is* pure, enlightening the eyes.

9 The fear of the LORD *is* clean, enduring for ever: the judgements of the LORD *are* true *and* righteous altogether.

10 More to be desired *are they* than gold, yea, than much fine gold: sweeter also than honey and the honeycomb.

11 Moreover by them is thy servant warned: *and* in keeping of them *there is* great reward.

12 Who can understand *his* errors? Cleanse thou me from secret *faults.*

13 Keep back thy servant also from presumptuous *sins;* let them not have dominion over me: then shall I be upright, and I shall be innocent from the great transgression.

14 Let the words of my mouth, and the meditation of my heart, be acceptable in thy sight, O LORD, my strength and my redeemer.

Psalm 20

To achieve victory.

To the chief Musician, A Psalm of David.

The LORD hear thee in the day of trouble; the name of God of Jacob defend thee;

2 Send thee help from the sanctuary, and strengthen thee out of Zion;

3 Remember all thy offerings, and accept thy burnt sacrifice; Selah.

4 Grant thee according to thine own heart, and fulfil all thy counsel.

5 We will rejoice in thy salvation, and in the name of our God we will set up our banners: the LORD fulfil all thy petitions.

6 Now know I that the LORD saveth his anointed; he will hear him from his holy heaven with the saving strength of his right hand.

7 Some *trust* in chariots, and some in horses; but we will remember the name of the LORD our God.

8 They are brought down and fallen: but we are risen, and stand upright.

9 Save, LORD: let the king hear us when we call.

Psalm 22

To invoke spiritual assistance.

To the chief Musician upon Aijeleth Shahar, A Psalm of David.

My God, my God, why hast thou forsaken me? *Why art thou* so far from helping me, *and from* the words of my roaring?

2 O my God, I cry in the daytime, but thou hearest not; and in the night season, and am not silent.

3 But thou *art* holy, *O thou* that inhabitest the praises of Israel.

4 Our fathers trusted in thee: they trusted, and thou didst deliver them.

5 They cried unto thee, and were delivered: they trusted in thee, and were not confounded.

6 But I *am* a worm, and no man; a reproach of men, and despised by the people.

7 All they that see me laugh me to scorn: they shoot out the lip, they shake the head, *saying,*

8 He trusted on the LORD *that* he would deliver him: let him deliver him, seeing he delighted in him.

9 But thou *art* he that took me out of the womb: thou didst make me hope *when I was* upon my mother's breasts.

10 I was cast upon thee from the womb: thou art my God from my mother's breasts.

11 Be not far from me; for trouble *is* near; for *there is* none to help.

12 Many bulls have compassed me: strong *bulls* of Bashan have beset me round.

13 They gaped upon me *with* their mouths, as a ravening and a roaring lion.

14 I am poured out like water, and all my bones are out of joint: my heart is like wax; it is melted in the midst of my bowels.

15 My strength is dried up like a potsherd; and my tongue cleaveth to my jaws; and thou hast brought me into the dust of death.

16 For dogs have compassed me: the assembly of the wicked have inclosed me: they pierced my hands and feet.

17 I may tell all my bones: they look *and* stare upon me.

18 They part my garments among them, and cast lots upon my vesture.

19 But be not thou far from me, O LORD: O my strength, haste thee to help me.

20 Deliver my soul from the sword; my darling from the power of the dog.

21 Save me from the lion's mouth: for thou hast heard me from the horns of the unicorns.

22 I will declare thy name unto my brethren: in the midst of the congregation will I praise thee.

23 Ye that fear the LORD, praise him; all ye the seed of Jacob, glorify him; and fear him, all ye seed of Israel.

24 For he hath not despised nor abhorred the affliction of the afflicted; neither hath he hid his face from him; but when he cried unto him, he heard.

25 My praise shall be of thee in the great congregation: I will pay my vows before them that fear him.

26 The meek shall eat and be satisfied: they shall praise the LORD that seek him: your heart shall live for ever.

27 All the ends of the world shall remember and turn unto the LORD: and all the kindreds of the nations shall worship before thee.

28 For the kingdom *is* the LORD's: and he is the governor among the nations.

29 All *they that be* fat upon the earth shall eat and worship: all they that go down to the dust shall bow before him: and none can keep alive his own soul.

30 A seed shall serve him; it shall be accounted to the LORD for a generation.

31 They shall come, and shall declare his righteousness unto a people that shall be born, that he hath done *this*.

Psalm 23

For self purification, and to overcome the forces of Chaos. The enumeration equates to Darkness in the lore of sacred geometry, for no structure built 23° or more above the equator receives light on its north wall. On the *Tree of Life,* *Psalm 23* corresponds to the Abyss (*Daath*); the realm of initiation.

A Psalm of David.

The LORD is my shepherd; I shall not want.

2 He maketh me to lie down in green pastures: he leadeth me besides still waters.

3 He restoreth my soul: he leadeth me in the paths of righteousness for his name's sake.

4 Yea, though I walk through the valley of the shadow of death, I will fear no evil: for thou *art* with me; thy rod and thy staff they comfort me.

5 Thou preparest a table before me in the presence of mine enemies: thou anointest my head with oil; my cup runneth over.

6 Surely goodness and mercy shall follow me all the days of my life: and I will dwell in the house of the LORD for ever.

Psalm 25

To overcome a bad habit. To change one's ways.

A Psalm of David.

Unto thee, O LORD, do I lift up my soul.

2 O my God, I trust in thee: let me be not ashamed, let not mine enemies triumph over me.

3 Yea, let none that wait on thee be ashamed: let them be ashamed which transgress without cause.

4 Shew me thy ways, O LORD; teach me thy paths.

5 Lead me in thy truth, and teach me: for thou *art* the God of my salvation; on thee do I wait all day.

6 Remember, O LORD, thy tender mercies and thy lovingkindnesses; for they *have been* ever of old.

7 Remember not the sins of my youth, nor my transgressions: according to thy mercy remember me for thy goodness' sake, O LORD.

8 Good and upright is the LORD: therefore will he teach sinners in the way.

9 The meek he will guide in judgment: and the meek will he teach his way.

10 All the paths of the LORD *are* mercy and truth unto such as keep his covenant and his testimonies.

11 For thy name's sake, O LORD, pardon mine iniquity; for it *is* great.

12 My foot standeth in an even place: in the congregations will I bless the LORD.

Psalm 30

To overcome ill health; a healing Psalm.

A Psalm and Song at the dedication of the house of David.

I will extol thee, O LORD; for thou hast lifted me up, and hast not made my foes to rejoice over me.

2 O LORD my God, I cried unto thee, and thou hast healed me.

3 O LORD, thou hast brought up my soul from the grave: thou hast kept me alive, that I should not go down into the pit.

4 Sing unto the LORD, O ye saints of his, and give thanks at the remembrance of his holiness.

5 For his anger *endureth but* a moment; in his favour *is* life: weeping may endure for a night, but joy *cometh* in the morning.

6 And in my prosperity I said, I shall never be moved.

7 LORD, by thy favour thou hast made my mountain to stand strong: thou didst hide thy face, *and* I was troubled.

8 I cried to thee, O LORD; and unto the LORD I made my supplication.

9 What profit *is there* in my blood, when I go down to the pit? Shall the dust praise thee? Shall it declare thy truth?

10 Hear, O LORD, and have mercy upon me: LORD thou be my helper.

11 Thou hast turned for me my mourning into dancing: thou hast put off my sackcloth, and girded me with gladness;

12 To the end that *my* glory may sing praise to thee, and not be silent. O LORD my God, I will give thanks unto thee for ever.

Psalm 31

To conquer fear.

To the chief Musician, A Psalm of David.

In thee, O LORD, do I put my trust; let me never be ashamed: deliver me in thy righteousness.

2 Bow down thin ear to me; deliver me speedily; be thou my strong rock, for an house of defence to save me.

3 For thou art my rock and my fortress; therefore for thy name's sake lead me, and guide me.

4 Pull me out of the net that they have laid privily for me: for thou *art* my strength.

5 Into thine hand I commit my spirit: thou hast redeemed me, O LORD God of truth.

6 I have hated them that regard lying vanities: but I trust in the LORD.

7 I will be glad and rejoice in thy mercy: for thou hast considered my trouble; thou hast known my soul in adversities;

8 And hast not shut me up into the hand of the enemy: thou hast set my feet in a large room.

9 Have mercy upon me, O LORD, for I am in trouble: mine eye is consumed with grief, *yea*, my soul and my belly.

10 For my life is spent with grief, and my years with sighing: my strength faileth because of mine iniquity, and my bones are consumed.

11 I was a reproach among all mine enemies, but especially among my neighbours, and a fear to mine acquaintance: that they did see me without fled from me.

12 I am forgotten as a dead man out of mind: I am like a broken vessel.

13 For I have heard the slander of many: fear *was* on every side: while they took counsel together against me, they devised to take away my life.

14 But I trusted in thee, O LORD: I said, Thou *art* my God.

15 My times are in thy hand: deliver me from the hand of mine enemies, and from them that persecute me.

16 Make thy face to shine upon thy servant: save me for thy mercies' sake.

17 Let me not be ashamed, O LORD; for I have called upon thee: let the wicked be ashamed, *and* let them be silent in the grave.

18 Let the lying lips be put to silence; which speak grievous things proudly and contemptuously against the righteous.

19 Oh how great is thy goodness, which thou hast laid up for them that fear thee; *which* thou hast wrought

for them that trust in thee before the sons of men!

20 Thou shalt hide them in the secret of the presence from the pride of man: thou shalt keep them secretly in a pavilion from the strife of tongues.

21 Blessed be the LORD: for he hath shewed me his marvelous kindness in a strong city.

22 For I said in my haste, I am cut off from before thine eyes: nevertheless thou heardest the voice of my supplications when I cried out to thee.

23 O love the LORD, all ye his saints: *for* the LORD preserveth the faithful, and plentifully rewardeth the proud doer.

24 Be of good courage, and he shall strengthen your heart, all ye that hope in the LORD.

Psalm 36

To stop gossip.

To the chief Musician, A Psalm of David the servant of the LORD.

The transgression of the wicked saith within my heart, *that there* is no fear of God before his eyes.

2 For he flattereth himself in his own eyes, until his iniquity be found to be hateful.

3 The words of his mouth *are* iniquity and deceit: he hath left off to be wise, *and* to do good.

4 He deviseth mischief upon his bed; he setteth himself in a way *that is* not good; he abhorreth not evil.

5 Thy mercy, O LORD, is in the heavens; *and* thy faithfulness *reacheth* unto the clouds.

6 Thy righteousness is like the great mountains; thy judgments are a great deep: O LORD, thou preservest man and beast.

7 How excellent *is* thy lovingkindness, O God! Therefore the children of men put their trust under the shadow of thy wings.

8 They shall be abundantly satisfied with the fatness of thy house; and thou shalt make them drink of the river of thy pleasures.

9 For with thee *is* the fountain of life: in thy light shall we see light.

10 O continue thy lovingkindness unto them that know thee; and thy righteousness to the upright in heart.

11 Let not the foot of pride come against me, and let not the hand of the wicked remove me.

12 There are the workers of iniquity fallen: they are cast down, and shall not be able to rise.

Psalm 37

To overcome fear.

A Psalm of David.

Fret not thyself because of evildoers, neither be thou envious against the workers of iniquity.

2 For they shall soon be cut down like the grass, and wither as the green herb.

3 Trust in the LORD, and do good; *so* shalt thou dwell in the land, and verily thou shalt be fed.

4 Delight thyself also in the LORD; and he shall give thee the desires of thin heart.

5 Commit thy way unto the LORD; trust also in him; and he shall bring *it* to pass.

6 And he shall bring forth thy righteousness as the light, and thy judgment in the noonday.

7 Rest in the LORD, and wait patiently for him: fret not thyself because of the man who bringeth wicked devices to pass.

8 Cease from anger, and forsake wrath: fret not thyself in any wise to do evil.

9 For evildoers shall be cut off: but those that wait upon the LORD, they shall inherit the earth.

10 For yet a little while, and the wicked *shall* not *be*: yea, thou shalt diligently consider his place, and it *shall* not *be*.

11 But the meek shall inherit the earth; and shall delight themselves in the abundance of peace.

12 The wicked plotteth against the just, and gnasheth upon him with his teeth,

13 The Lord shall laugh at him: for he seeth that his day is coming.

14 The wicked have drawn out the sword, and have bent their bow, to cast down the poor and needy, *and* to slay such as be of upright conversation.

15 Their sword shall enter their own heart, and their bows shall be broken.

16 A little that a righteous man hath *is* better than the riches of the many wicked.

17 For the arms of the wicked shall be broken: but the LORD upholdeth the righteous.

18 The LORD knoweth the days of the upright: and their inheritance shall be for ever.

19 They shall not be ashamed in the evil time: and in the days of famine they shall be satisfied.

20 But the wicked shall perish, and the enemies of the LORD *shall* be as the fat of lambs: they shall consume; into smoke shall they consume away.

21 The wicked borroweth, and payeth not again: but the righteous sheweth mercy, and giveth.

22 For *such as be* blessed of him shall inherit the earth; and *they that be* cursed of him shall be cut off.

23 The steps of the good man are ordered by the LORD: and he delighteth in his way.

24 Though he fall, he shall not be utterly cast down: for the LORD upholdeth *him with* his hand.

25 I have been young, and *now* am old; yet have I not seen the righteous forsaken, nor his seed begging bread.

26 *He is* ever merciful, and lendeth; and his seed *is* blessed.

27 Depart from evil, and do good; and dwell for evermore.

28 For the LORD loveth judgment, and forsaketh not his saints; they are preserved for ever: but the seed of the wicked shall be cut off.

29 The righteous shall inherit the land, and dwell therein forever.

30 The mouth of the righteous speaketh wisdom, and his tongue talketh of judgment.

31 The law of his God *is* in his heart; none of his steps shall slide.

32 The wicked watcheth the righteous, and seeketh to slay him.

33 The LORD will not leave him in his hand, nor condemn him when he is judged.

34 Wait on the LORD, and keep his way, and he shall exalt thee to inherit the land: when the wicked are cut off, thou shalt see *it*.

35 I have seen the wicked in great power, and spreading himself like a green bay tree.

36 Yet he passed away, and, lo, he *was* not: yea, I sought him, but he could not be found.

37 Mark the perfect *man*, and behold the upright: for the end of *that* man *is* peace.

38 But the transgressors shall be destroyed together: the end of the wicked shall be cut off.

39 But the salvation of the righteous *is* of the LORD: *he is* their strength in the time of trouble.

40 And the LORD shall help them, and deliver them: he shall deliver them from the wicked, and save them, because they trust in him.

Psalm 38

Overcoming illness, and regaining health.

A Psalm of david, to bring to remembrance.

O LORD, rebuke me not in thy wrath: neither chasten me in thy hot displeasure.

2 For thine arrows stick fast in me, and thy hand presseth me sore.

3 *There is* no soundness in my flesh because of thine anger; neither *is there* any rest in my bones because of my sin.

4 For mine iniquities are gone over mine head: as an heavy burden they are too heavy for me.

5 My wounds stink *and* are corrupt because of my foolishness.

6 I am troubled; I am bowed down greatly; I go mourning all day long.

7 For my loins are filled with loathsome *disease*: and *there* is no soundness in my flesh.

8 I am feeble and sore broken: I have roared by reason of the disquietness of my heart.

9 Lord, all my desire *is* before thee; and my groaning is not hid from thee.

10 My heart panteth, my strength faileth me: as for the light of mine eyes, it also is gone from me.

11 My lovers and my friends stand aloof from my sore; and my kinsmen stand afar off.

12 They also that seek after my life lay snares for me: and they that seek my hurt speak mischievous things, and imagine deceits all day long.

13 But I, as a deaf *man*, heard not; and *I was* as a dumb man *that* openeth not his mouth.

14 Thus I was a man that heareth not, and in whose mouth *are* no reproofs.

15 For in thee, O LORD, do I hope: thou wilt hear, O Lord my God.

16 For I said, Hear me, lest otherwise they should rejoice over me: when my foot slippeth, they magnify *themselves* against me.

17 For I *am* ready to halt, and my sorrow is continually before me.

18 For I will declare mine iniquity; I will be sorry for my sin.

19 But mine enemies are lively, and they are strong: and they that hate me wrongfully are multiplied.

20 They also that render evil for good are mine adversaries; because I follow *the thing that* good *is*.

21 Forsake me not, O LORD: O my God, be not far from me.

22 Make haste to help me, O Lord my salvation.

Psalm 41

To obtain money.

To the chief Musician, A Psalm of David.

Blessed *is* he that considereth the poor: the LORD will deliver him in time of trouble.

2 The LORD will preserve him, and keep him alive; and he shall be blessed upon the earth: *and* thou wilt not deliver him unto the will of his enemies.

3 The LORD will strengthen him upon the bed of languishing: thou wilt make all his bed in sickness.

4 I said, LORD, be merciful unto me: heal my soul; for I have sinned against thee.

5 Mine enemies speak evil of me, When shall he die, and his name perish?

6 And if he come to see *me*, he speaketh vanity: his heart gathereth iniquity to itself; *when* he goeth abroad, he telleth *it*.

7 All that hate me whisper together against me: against me do they devise my hurt.

8 An evil disease, say they, cleaveth fast unto him: and now that he lieth he shall rise up no more.

9 Yea, mine own familiar friend, in whom I trusted, which did eat of my bread, has lifted up *his* heel against me.

10 But thou, O LORD, be merciful unto me, because mine enemy doth not triumph over me.

12 And as for me, thou upholdest me in mine integrity, and settest me before thy face for ever.

13 Blessed *be* the LORD God of Israel from everlasting, and to everlasting. Amen, and Amen.

Psalm 59

To be rid of enemies.

To the chief Musician, Al-taschith, Michtam of David; when Saul sent, and they watched the house to kill him.

Deliver me from mine enemies, O my God: defend against them that rise up against me.

2 Deliver me from the workers of iniquity, and save me from bloody men.

3 For, lo, they lie in wait for my soul: the mighty are gathered against me; not *for* my transgression, not *for* my sin, O LORD.

4 They run and prepare themselves without *my* fault: awake to help me, and behold.

5 Thou therefore, O LORD God of hosts, the God of Israel, awake to visit all the heathen: be not merciful to any wicked transgressors. Selah.

6 They return at evening: they make a noise like a dog, and go round about the city.

7 Behold, they belch out with their mouth: swords *are* in their lips: for who, *say they*, doth hear?

8 But thou, O LORD, shalt laugh at them; thou shalt have all the heathen in derision.

9 Because of his strength will I wait upon thee: for God *is* my defence.

10 The God of my mercy shall prevent me: God shall let me see *my desire* upon mine enemies.

11 Slay them not, lest my people forget: scatter them by thy power; and bring them down, O Lord our shield.

12 *For* the sin of their mouth *and* the words of their lips let them even be taken in their pride: and for cursing and lying *which* they speak.

13 Consume *them* in wrath, consume *them*, that they *may* not *be*: and let them know that God ruleth in Jacob unto the ends of the earth. Selah.

14 And at evening let them return; *and* let them make a noise like a dog, and go round about the city.

15 Let them wander up and down for meat, and grudge if they be not satisfied.

16 But I will sing of thy power; yea, I will sing aloud of thy mercy in the morning: for thou hast been my defence and refuge in the day of my trouble.

17 Unto thee, O my strength, will I sing: for God is my defence, and the God of my mercy.

Psalm 61

To sell property, or to move home.

To the chief Musician upon Neginah, A Psalm of David.

Hear my cry, O God; attend unto my prayer.

2 From the end of the earth will I cry unto thee, when my heart is overwhelmed: lead me to the rock *that* is higher than I.

3 For thou hast been a shelter for me, *and* a strong tower from the enemy.

4 I will abide in thy tabernacle for ever: I will trust in the covert of thy wings. Selah.

5 For thou, O God, hast heard my vows: thou hast given *me* the heritage of those that fear my name.

6 Thou wilt prolong the king's life: *and* his years as many generations.

7 He shall abide before God for ever: O prepare mercy and truth, *which* may preserve him.

8 So will I sing praise unto thy name for ever, that I may daily perform my vows.

Psalm 63

To arouse envy in others.

A Psalm of David, when he was in the wilderness of Judah.

O God, thou art my God; early will I seek thee: my soul thirsteth for thee, my flesh longeth for thee in the dry and thirsty land, where no water is;

2 To see thy power and thy glory, so as I have seen thee in the sanctuary.

3 Because thy lovingkindness is better than life, my lips shall praise thee.

4 Thus I will bless thee while I live: I will lift up my hands in thy name.

5 My soul shall be satisfied as *with* marrow and fatness; and my mouth shall praise *thee* with joyful lips.

6 When I remember thee upon my bed, and meditate on thee in the *night* watches.

7 Because thou hast been my help, therefore in the shadow of thy wings will I rejoice.

8 My soul followeth hard after thee: thy right hand upholdeth me.

9 But those *that* seek my soul, to destroy *it*, shall go into the lower parts of the earth.

10 They shall fall by the sword: they shall be a portion for foxes.

11 But the king shall rejoice in God; every one that sweareth by him shall glory: but the mouth of them that speak lies shall be stopped.

Psalm 65

To accomplish goals.

To the chief Musician, A Psalm of David.

Praise waiteth for thee, O God, in Sion: and unto thee shall the vow be performed.

2 O thou that hearest prayer, unto thee shall all flesh come.

3 Iniquities prevail against me: *as for* our transgressions, thou shalt purge them away.

4 Blessed *is the man whom* thou choosest, and causes to approach *unto thee, that* he may dwell in thy courts: we shall be satisfied with the goodness of thy house, *even* of thy holy temple.

5 By terrible things in righteousness wilt thou answer us, O God of our salvation; who art the confidence of all the ends of the earth, and of them that are afar off on the sea:

6 Which by his strength setteth fast the mountains; *being* girded with power:

7 Which stilleth the noise of the seas, the noise of their waves, and the tumult of the people.

8 They also that dwell in the uttermost parts are afraid at thy tokens: thou makest the outgoings of the morning and evening to rejoice.

9 Thou visitest the earth, and waterest it: thou greatly enrichest it with the river of God, *which* is full of water: thou preparest them corn, when thou hast so provided for it.

10 Thou waterest the ridges thereof abundently: thou settlest the furrows thereof: thou makest it soft with showers: thou blessest the spring thereof.

11 Thou crownest the year with thy goodness: and thy paths drop fatness.

12 They drop upon the pastures of the wilderness: and the little hills rejoice on every side.

13 The pastures are closed with flocks; the valleys also are covered over with corn; they shout for joy, they also sing.

Psalm 70

To send back a curse, or other trouble. To arouse anger, jealousy, and confusion.

To the chief Musician, A Psalm of David, to bring to remembrance.

*M*ake haste, O God, to deliver me; make haste to help me, O LORD.

2 Let them be ashamed and confounded that seek after my soul: let them be turned backward, and put to confusion, that desire my hurt.

3 Let them be turned back for a reward of their shame that say, Aha, aha.

4 Let all those that seek thee rejoice and be glad in thee: and let such as love thy salvation say continually, Let God be magnified.

5 But I *am* poor and needy: make haste unto me, O God: thou *art* my help and my deliverer; O LORD, make no tarrying.

Psalm 71

Protection against curses.

In thee, O LORD, do I put my trust: let me never be put to confusion.

2 Deliver me in thy righteousness, and cause me to escape: incline thine ear unto me, and save me.

3 Be thou my strong habitation, whereunto I may continually resort: thou hast given commandment to save me; for thou *art* my rock and my fortress.

4 Deliver me, O my God, out of the hand of the wicked, out of the hand of the unrighteous and cruel man.

5 For thou *art* my hope, O Lord GOD: *thou art* my trust from my youth.

6 By thee have I been holden up from the womb: thou art he that took me out from my mother's bowels: my praise *shall be* continually of thee.

7 I am as a wonder unto many; but thou *art* my strong refuge.

8 Let my mouth be filled with thy praise *and with* thy honour all the day.

9 Cast me not off in the time of old age; forsake me not when my strength faileth.

10 For mine enemies speak against me and they that lay in wait for my soul take counsel together.

11 Saying, God hath forsaken him: persecute and take him; for *there* is none to deliver *him*.

12 O God, be not far from me: O my God, make haste for my help.

13 Let them be confounded *and* consumed that are adversaries to my soul; let them be covered *with* reproach and dishonour that seek my hurt.

14 But I will hope continually, and will yet praise thee more and more.

15 My mouth shall shew forth thy righteousness *and* thy salvation all the day; for I know not the bumbers *thereof.*

16 I will go in the strength of the Lord GOD: I will make mention of thy righteousness, *even* of thine only.

17 O God, thou hast taught me from my youth: and hitherto have I declared thy wondrous works.

18 Now also I am old and greyheaded, O God, forsake me not; until I have shewed thy strength unto *this* generation.

19 Thy righteousness also, O God, is very high, who hast done great things: O God, who *is* like unto thee!

20 *Thou*, which hast shewed me great and sore troubles, shalt quicken me again, and shalt bring me up again from the depths of the earth.

21 Thou shalt increase my greatness, and comfort me on every side.

22 I will praise thee with the psaltery, even *thy* truth, O my God: unto thee will I sing with the harp, O thou Holy One of Israel.

23 My lips shall greatly rejoice when I sing unto thee; and my soul, which thou hast redeemed.

24 My tongue also shall talk of thy righteousness all the day long: for they are confounded, for they are brought unto shame, that seek my hurt.

Psalm 85

To heal a rift.

To the chief Musician, A Psalm for the sons of Korah.

Lord, thou hast been favourable unto thy land: thou hast brought back the captivity of Jacob.

2 Thou hast forgiven the iniquity of thy people, thou hast covered all their sin. Selah.

3 Thou hast taken away all thy wrath: thou hast turned thyself from the fierceness of thine anger.

4 Turn us, O God of our salvation, and cause thine anger toward us to cease.

5 Wilt thou be angry with us for ever? Wilt thou draw out thine anger to all generations?

6 Wilt thou not revive us again: that thy people may rejoice in thee?

7 Shew us thy mercy, O LORD, and grant us thy salvation.

8 I will hear what God the LORD will speak: for he will speak peace unto his people, and to his saints: but let them not turn again to folly.

9 Surely his salvation *is* nigh them that fear him; that glory may dwell in our land.

10 Mercy and truth are met together; righteousness and peace have kissed *each other.*

11 Truth shall spring out of the earth; and righteousness shall look down from heaven.

12 Yea, the LORD shall give that which is good; and our land shall yield her increase.

13 Righteousness shall go before him; and shall set *us* in the way of his steps.

Psalm 92

To gain promotion.

A Psalm or Song for the sabbath day.

It is a good *thing* to give thanks unto the LORD, and to sing praises unto thy name, O most High.

2 To shew forth thy lovingkindness in the morning, and thy faithfulness every night,

3 Upon an instrument of ten strings, and upon the psaltery; upon the harp with a solemn sound.

4 For thou, LORD, hast made me glad through thy work; I will triumph in the works of thy hands.

5 O LORD, how great are thy works! *And* thy thoughts are very deep.

6 A brutish man knoweth not; neither doth a fool understand this.

7 When the wicked spring as the grass, and when all the workers of iniquity do flourish; *it is* that they shall be destroyed for evermore.

8 But thou, LORD, *art most* high for evermore.

9 For, lo, thine enemies, O LORD, for, lo, thine enemies shall perish; all the workers of iniquity shall be scattered.

10 But my horn shalt thou exalt like *the horn* of an unicorn: I shall be anointed with fresh oil.

11 Mine eye also shall see *my desire* on mine enemies, *and* mine ears shall hear *my desire* of the wicked that rise up against me.

12 The righteous shall flourish like the palm tree: he shall grow like the cedar in Lebanon.

13 Those that be planted in the house of the LORD shall flourish in the courts of our God.

14 They shall bring forth fruit in old age; they shall be fat and flourishing;

15 To shew that the LORD is upright; *he is* my rock, and *there* is no unrighteousness in him.

Psalm 93

To curse an enemy.

The Lord reigneth, he is clothed with majesty; the LORD is clothed with strength, *wherewith* he hath girded himself: the world also is established, that it cannot be moved.

2 Thy throne *is* established of old: thou *art* from everlasting.

3 The floods have lifted up, O LORD, the floods have lifted up their voice; the floods lift up their waves.

4 The LORD on high is mightier than the noise of many waters, *yea, than* the mighty waves of the sea.

5 Thine testimonies are very sure; holiness becometh thine house, O LORD, for ever.

Psalm 109

To turn back curses, and destroy their sender. A most powerful Psalm in times of spiritual warfare.

To the chief Musician, A Psalm of David.

Hold not thy peace, O God of my praise;

2 For the mouth of the wicked and the mouth of the deceitful are opened against me: they have spoken against me with a lying tongue.

3 They compassed me about also with words of hatred; and fought against me without a cause.

4 For my love they are my adversaries: but I give myself unto prayer.

5 And they have rewarded me evil for good, and hatred for my love.

6 Set thou a wicked man over him: and let Satan stand at his right hand.

7 When he shall be judged, let him be condemned: and let his prayer become sin.

8 Let his days be few; *and* let another take his office.

9 Let his children be fatherless, and his wife a widow.

10 Let his children be continually vagabonds, and beg: let them seek their bread also out of their desolate places.

11 Let the extortioner catch all that he hath; and let strangers spoil his labour.

12 Let there be none to extend mercy unto him: neither let there be any to favour his fatherless children.

13 Let his posterity be cut off; *and* in the generation following let their name be blotted out.

14 Let the iniquity of his fathers be remembered with the LORD; and let not the sin of his mother be blotted out.

15 Let them be before the LORD continually, that he may cut off the memory of them from the earth.

16 Because that he remembered not to shew mercy, but persecuted the poor and needy man, that he might even slay the broken in heart.

17 As he loved cursing, so let it come unto him: as he delighted not in blessing, so let it be far from him.

18 As he clothed himself with cursing like as with his garment, so let it come into his bowels like water, and like oil into his bones.

19 Let it be unto him as the garments *which* covereth him, and for a girdle wherewith he is girded continually.

20 Let this be the reward of mine adversaries from the LORD, and of them that speak evil against my soul.

21 But do thou for me, O God the Lord, for thy name's sake: because thy mercy *is* good, deliver thou me.

22 For I am poor and needy, and my heart is wounded within me.

23 I am gone like the shadow when it declineth: I am tossed up and down as the locust.

24 My knees are weak through fasting; and my flesh faileth of fatness.

25 I became also a reproach unto them: *when* they looked upon me they shaked their heads.

26 Help me, O LORD my God: O save me according to thy mercy:

27 That they may know that this *is* thy hand; *that* thou, LORD, hast done it.

28 Let them curse, but bless thou: when they arise, let them be ashamed; but let thy servant rejoice.

29 Let mine adversaries be clothed with shame, and let them cover themselves with their own confusion, as with a mantle.

30 I will greatly praise the LORD with my mouth; yea, I will praise him among the multitude.

31 For he shall stand at the right hand of the poor, to save *him* from those that condemn his soul.

Psalm 117

To learn the truth.

O praise the LORD, all ye nations: praise him, all ye people.

2 For his merciful kindness is great toward us: and the truth of the LORD *endureth* for ever. Praise ye the LORD.

Psalm 119

Psalm 119 - itself the longest chapter in the entire *Bible* - is amongst the acrostic (alphabetical) Psalms, divided into 22 Stanzas of 8 lines, each of which begins with the successive letters of the Hebrew alphabet, and thus relating to the 22 Paths between the Sephiroth upon the *Tree of Life*. Each stanza is ordained with its own powers as follows;

To assist in maintaining integrity. Corresponds to the *11th Path*, above the Abyss (*Daath*), between *Kether* and *Hokmah*.

ALEPH

Blessed *are* the undefiled in the way, who walk in the law of the LORD.

2 Blessed *are* they that keep his testimonies, *and that* seek him with their whole heart.

3 They also do no iniquity: they walk in his ways.

4 Thou hast commanded *us* to keep thy precepts diligently.

5 O that my ways were directed to keep thy statutes!

6 Then shall I not be ashamed, when I have respect unto all thy commandments.

7 I will praise thee with uprightness of heart, when I shall have learned thy righteous judgments.

8 I will keep thy statutes: O forsake me not utterly.

For self purification. Corresponds to the *12th Path*, above the Abyss (*Daath*), between *Kether* and *Binah*.

BETH

9 Wherewithal shall a young man cleanse his way? By taking heed *thereto* according to thy word.

10 With my whole heart have I sought thee: O let me not wander from thy commandments.

11 Thy word have I hid in my heart, that I might not sin against thee.

12 Blessed *art* thou, O LORD: teach me thy statutes.

13 With my lips have I declared all the judgments of thy mouth.

14 I have rejoiced in the way of thy testimonies, as *much* as in all riches.

15 I will meditate in thy precepts, and have respect unto thy ways.

16 I will delight myself in thy statutes: I will not forget thy word.

To attract wealth. Corresponds to the *15th Path*, traversing the Abyss (*Daath*) between *Kether* and *Tiphareth*.

GIMEL

17 Deal bountifully with thy servant, *that* I may live, and keep thy word.

18 Open thou mine eyes, that I may behold wondrous things out of thy law.

19 I *am* a stranger in the earth: hide not thy commandments from me.

20 My soul breaketh for the longing *that it hath* unto thy judgments at all times.

21 Thou hast rebuked the proud *that are* cursed, which do err from thy commandments.

22 Remove from me reproach and contempt; for I have kept thy testimonies.

23 Princes also did sit *and* speak against me: *but* thy servant did meditate in thy statutes.

24 Thy testimonies also *are* my delight *and* my counsellers.

To increase wisdom. Corresponds to the *14th Path*, traversing the Abyss (*Daath*) between *Binah* and *Hokmah*.

DALETH

25 My soul cleaveth unto the dust: quicken thou me according to thy word.

26 I have declared my ways, and thou heardest me: teach me thy statutes.

27 Make me to understand the way of thy precepts: so shall I talk of thy wondrous works.

28 My soul melteth for heaviness: strengthen thou me according to thy word.

29 Remove from me the way of lying: and grant me thy laws graciously.

30 I have chosen the way of truth: thy judgments have laid *before me*.

31 I have stuck unto thy testimonies: O LORD, put me not to shame.

32 I will run the way of thy commandments, when thou shalt enlarge my heart.

To change one's habits and ways. Corresponds to the *11th Path*, between *Kether* and *Tiphareth*.

HEH

33 Teach me, O LORD, the way of thy statutes; and I shall keep it *unto* the end.

34 Give me understanding, and I shall keep thy law; yea, I shall observe it with *my* whole heart.

35 Make me to go in the path of thy commandments; for therein do I delight.

36 Incline my heart unto thy testimonies, and not to covetousness.

37 Turn away mine eyes from beholding vanity; *and* quicken thou me in thy way.

38 Turn away my reproach which I fear: for thy judgments *are* good.

39 Turn away my reproach which I fear: for thy judgments *are* good.

40 Behold, I have longed after thy precepts: quicken me in thy righteousness.

To call for help and aid, and to cause others to serve you willingly. Corresponds to the *16th Path*, between *Hokmah* and *Hesed*.

VAU

41 Let thy mercies come also unto me, O LORD, *even* thy salvation, according to thy word.

42 So shall I have wherewith to answer him that reproacheth me: for I trust in thy word.

43 And take not he word of truth utterly out of my mouth; for I trust in thy word.

44 So shall I keep thy law continually for ever and ever.

45 And I will walk at liberty: for I seek thy precepts.

46 I will speak of thy testimonies also before kings, and will not be ashamed.

47 And I will delight myself in thy commandments, which I have loved.

48 My hands also will I lift up unto thy commandments, which I have loved; and I will meditate on thy statutes.

Turning away from addiction and self destruction. Corresponds to the *17th Path*, between *Binah* and *Tiphareth*.

ZAIN

49 Remember the word unto thy servant, upon which thou hast caused me to hope.

50 This is my comfort in my affliction: for thy word has quickened me.

51 The proud have me greatly in derision: *yet* have I not declined from thy law.

52 I remembered thy judgments of old, O LORD; and have comforted myself.

53 Horror hath taken hold upon me because of the wicked that forsake thy law.

54 Thy statutes have been my songs in the house of my pilgrimage.

55 I have remembered thy name, O LORD, in the night, and have kept thy law.

56 This I had, because I kept thy precepts.

To overcome isolation. Corresponds to the *18th Path*, between *Binah* and *Geburah*.

CHETH

57 Thou art my portion, O LORD: I have said that I would keep thy words.

58 I intreated thy favour with *my* whole heart: be merciful unto me according to thy word.

59 I thought on my ways, and turned my feet unto thy testimonies.

60 I made haste, and delayed not to keep thy commandments.

61 The bands of the wicked have robbed me: *but* I have not forgotten thy law.

62 At midnight I will rise to give thanks unto thee because of thy righteous judgments.

63 I *am* a companion of all *them* that fear thee, and of them that keep thy precepts.

64 The earth, O LORD, is full of thy mercy: teach me thy statutes.

To overcome madness, confusion, and anxiety. Corresponds to the *19th Path*, between *Hesed* and *Geburah*.

TETH

65 Thou hast dealt well with thy servant, O LORD, according to thy word.

66 Teach me good judgment and knowledge: for I have believed thy commandments.

67 Before I was afflicted I went astray: but now have I kept thy word.

68 Thou *art* good, and doest good; teach me thy statutes.

69 The proud have forged a lie against me: *but* I will keep thy precepts with *my* whole heart.

70 Their heart is as fat as grease; *but* I delight in thy law.

71 It is good for me that I have been afflicted; that I might learn thy statutes.

72 The law of thy mouth *is* better unto me than thousands of gold and silver.

To gain employment. Corresponds to the *20th Path*, between *Hesed* and *Tiphareth*.

YOD

73 Thy hands have made me and fashioned me; give me understanding, that I may learn thy commandments.

74 They that fear thee will be glad when they see me; because I have hoped in thy word.

75 I know, O LORD, that thy judgments *are* right, and *that* thou in faithfulness hast afflicted me.

76 Let, I pray thee, thy merciful kindness be for my comfort, according to thy word unto thy servant.

77 Let thy tender mercies come unto me, that I may live: for thy law *is* my delight.

78 Let the proud be ashamed; for they dealt perversely with me without a cause: *but* I will meditate in thy precepts.

79 Let those that fear thee turn unto me, and those that have known thy testimonies.

80 Let my heart be sound in thy statutes; that I be not ashamed.

To overcome persecution. Corresponds to the *21st Path*, between *Hesed* and *Netzach*.

KAPH

81 My soul fainteth for thy salvation: *but* I hope in thy word.

82 Mine eyes fail for thy word, saying, When wilt thou comfort me?

83 For I am become like a bottle in the smoke; *yet* do I not forget thy statutes.

84 How many are the days of thy servant? When wilt thou execute judgment on them that persecute me?

85 The proud have digged pits for me, which *are* not after thy law.

86 All thy commandments are faithful: they persecute me wrongfully; help thou me.

87 They had almost consumed me upon earth; but I forsook not thy precepts.

88 Quicken me after thy lovingkindness; so I shall keep the testimony of thy mouth.

For compassion in victory. Corresponds to the *22nd Path*, between *Geburah* and *Tiphareth*.

LAMED

89 For ever, O LORD, thy word is settled in heaven.

90 Thy faithfulness is unto all generations: thou hast established the earth, and it abideth.

91 They continue this day according to thine ordinances: for all *are* thy servants.

92 Unless thy law *had been* my delights, I should then have perished in mine affliction.

93 I will never forget thy precepts: for with them thou hast quickened me.

94 I *am* thine, save me; for I have sought thy precepts.

95 The wicked have waited for me to destroy me: *but* I will consider thy testimonies.

96 I have seen an end of all perfection: *but* thy commandment is exceeding broad.

To gain wisdom. Corresponds to the *23rd Path*, between *Geburah* and *Hod*.

MEMM

97 O how love I thy law! It *is* my meditation all the day.

98 Thou through thy commandments hast made me wiser than mine enemies: for they *are* ever with me.

99 I have more understanding than all my teachers: for thy testimonies *are* my meditation.

100 I understand more than the ancients, because I keep thy precepts.

101 I have refrained my feet from every evil way, that I may keep thy word.

102 I have not departed from thy judgments: for thou hast taught me.

103 How sweet are thy words unto my taste! *Yea, sweeter* than honey to my mouth.

104 Through thy precepts I get understanding: therefore I hate every false way.

To improve communication and understanding. Corresponds to the *24th Path*, between *Tiphareth* and *Netzach*.

NUN

105 Thy word *is* a lamp unto my feet, and a light unto my path.

106 I have sworn, and I will perform *it*, that I will keep thy righteous judgments.

107 I am afflicted very much: quicken me, O LORD, according to thy word.

108 Accept, I beseech thee, the freewill offerings of my mouth, O LORD, and teach me thy judgments.

109 My soul *is* continually in my hand: yet do I not forget thy law.

110 The wicked have laid a snare for me: yet I erred not from thy precepts.

111 Thy testimonies have I taken as an heritage for ever: for they are the rejoicing of my heart.

112 I have inclined mine heart to perform thy statutes always, *even unto* the end.

To gain confidence. Corresponds to the *25th Path*, between *Tiphareth* and *Yesod*.

SAMECH

113 I hate *vain* thoughts: but the law do I love.

114 Thou *art* my hiding place and my shield: I hope in thy word.

115 Depart from me, ye evildoers: for I will keep the commandments of my God.

116 Uphold me according unto thy word, that I may live: and let me not be ashamed of my hope.

117 Hold thou me up, and I shall be safe: and I will have respect unto thy statutes continually.

118 Thou hast trodden down all them that err from thy statutes: for their deceit *is* falsehood.

119 Thou puttest away all the wicked of the earth *like* dross: therefore I love thy testimonies.

120 My flesh trembleth for fear of thee; and I am afraid of thy judgments.

To gain reward for one's efforts. Corresponds to the *26th Path*, between *Tiphareth* and *Hod*.

AYIN

121 I have done judgment and justice: leave me not to mine oppressors.

122 Be surety for thy servant for good: let not the proud oppress me.

123 Mine eyes fail for thy salvation, and for the word of thy righteousness.

124 Deal with thy servant according unto thy mercy, and teach me thy statutes.

125 I *am* thy servant; give me understanding, that I may know thy testimonies.

126 *It is* time for *thee*, LORD, to work: *for* they have made void thy law.

127 Therefore I love thy commandments above gold; yea, above fine gold.

128 Therefore I esteem all *thy* precepts *concerning* all *things to be* right; *and* I hate every false way.

To find a path through doubt. Corresponds to the *27th Path*, between *Hod* and *Netzach*.

PEH

129 Thy testimonies *are* wonderful: therefore doeth my soul keep them.

130 The entrance of thy words giveth light: it giveth understanding unto the simple.

131 I opened my mouth, and panted: for I longed for thy commandments.

132 Look thou upon me, and be merciful unto me, as thou usest to do unto those that love thy name.

133 Order my steps in thy word: and let not any iniquity have dominion over me.

134 Deliver me from the oppression of man: so I will keep thy precepts.

135 Make thy face to shine upon thy servant; and teach me thy statutes.

136 Rivers of water run down mine eyes, because they keep not thy law.

To overcome fear and anxiety. Corresponds to the *28th Path*, between *Netzach* and *Yesod*.

TZADDI

137 Righteous *art* thou, O LORD, and upright are thy judgments.

138 Thy testimonies *that* thou hast commanded are righteous and very faithful.

139 My zeal hath consumed me, because mine enemies have forgotten thy words.

140 Thy word *is* very pure: therefore thy servant loveth it.

141 I *am* small and despised: yet do not I forget thy precepts.

142 Thy righteousness *is* an everlasting righteousness, and thy law *is* the truth.

143 Trouble and anguish have taken hold on me: yet thy commandments *are* my delights.

144 The righteousness of thy testimonies *is* everlasting: give me understanding, and I shall live.

To overcome confusion. Corresponds to the *29th Path*, between *Netzach* and *Malkuth*.

QUOPH

145 I cried with *my* whole heart; hear me, O LORD: I will keep thy statutes.

146 I cried unto thee; save me, and I shall keep thy testimonies.

147 I prevented the dawning of the morning, and cried: I hoped in thy word.

148 Mine eyes prevent the night watches, that I might meditate in thy word.

149 Hear my voice according unto thy lovingkindness: O LORD, quicken me according to thy judgment.

150 They draw nigh that follow after mischief: they are far from thy law.

151 Thou *art* near, O LORD; and all thy commandments *are* truth.

152 Concerning thy testimonies, I have known of old that thou hast founded them for ever.

To overcome illness. Corresponds to the *30th Path*, between *Kether* and *Hokmah*.

RESH

153 Consider mine affliction, and deliver me: for I do not forget the law.

154 Plead my cause, and deliver me: quicken me according to thy word.

155 Salvation *is* far from the wicked: for they seek not thy statutes.

156 Great *are* thy tender mercies, O LORD: quicken me according to thy judgments.

157 Many *are* my persecutors and mine enemies; yet do I not decline from thy testimonies.

158 I beheld the transgressors, and was grieved; because they kept not thy word.

159 Consider how I love thy precepts: quicken me, O LORD, according to thy lovingkindness.

160 Thy word *is* true *from* the beginning: and every one of thy righteous judgments *endureth* forever.

To remove obstacles. Corresponds to the *31st Path*, between *Hod* and *Malkuth*.

SHIN

161 Princes have persecuted me without a cause: but my heart standeth in awe of thy word.

162 I rejoice at thy word, as one that findeth great spoil.

163 I hate and abhor lying: *but* thy law do I love.

164 Seven times a day do I praise thee because of thy righteous judgments.

165 Great peace have they which love thy law: and nothing shall offend them.

166 LORD, I have hoped for thy salvation, and done thy commandments.

167 My soul hath kept thy testimonies; and I love them exceedingly.

168 I have kept thy precepts and thy testimonies: for all my ways *are* before thee.

To forgive other's errors. Corresponds to the *32nd Path*, between *Netzach* and *Malkuth*.

TAU

169 Let my cry come near before thee, O LORD: give me understanding according to thy word.

170 Let my supplications come before thee: deliver me according to thy word.

171 My lips shall utter praise, when thou hast taught me of thy statutes.

172 My tongue shall speak thy words: for all thy commandments *are* righteousness.

173 Let thine hand help me; for I have chosen thy precepts.

174 I have longed for thy salvation, O LORD; and thy law *is* my delight.

175 Let my soul live, and it shall praise thee; and let thy judgments help me.

176 I have gone astray like a lost sheep; seek thy servant; for I do not forget thy commandments.

Psalm 130

To gain dominion over others.

A Song of degrees.

Out of the depths have I cried unto thee, O LORD.

2 Lord, hear my voice: let thine ears be attentive to the voice of my supplications.

3 If thou, LORD, shouldest mark iniquities, O Lord, who shall stand?

4 But *there is* forgiveness with thee, that thou mayest be feared.

5 I wait for the LORD, my soul doth wait, and in his word do I hope.

6 My soul *waiteth* for the Lord more than they that watch for the morning: I say, more than they that watch for the morning.

7 Let Israel hope in the LORD: for with the LORD *there is* mercy, and with him *is* plenteous redemption.

8 And he shall redeem Israel from all his iniquities.

Psalm 133

To gain new friends.

A Song of degrees of David.

Behold, how good and how pleasant *it is* for brethren to dwell together in unity!

2 *It is* like the precious ointments upon the head, that ran down upon the beard, *even* Aaron's beard: that went down to the skirts of his garments.

3 As the dew of Hermon, and as the dew that descended upon the mountains of Zion: for there the LORD commanded the blessing, *even* life for evermore.

Psalm 137

To overcome oppression.

By the rivers of Babylon, there we sat down, yea we wept, when we remembered Zion.

2 We hanged our harps upon the willows in the midst thereof.

3 For there they that carried us away captive required of us a song; and they that wasted us *required of us* mirth, *saying*, Sing us one of the songs of Zion.

4 How shall we sing the LORD's song in a strange land?

5 If I forget thee, O Jerusalem, let my right hand forget *her cunning.*

6 If I do not remember thee, let my tongue cleave to the roof of my mouth; if I prefer not Jerusalem above my chief joy.

7 Remember, O LORD, the children of Edom in the day of Jerusalem; who said, Rase *it,* rase *it, even* to the foundation thereof.

8 O daughter of Babylon, who art to be destroyed; happy *shall he be,* that rewardeth thee as thou hast served us.

9 Happy *shall he be*, that taketh and dasheth thy little ones against the stones.

Psalm 138

To attract love.

A Psalm of David.

I will praise thee with my whole heart: before the gods will I sing praise unto thee.

2 I will worship toward thy holy temple, and praise thy name for thy lovingkindness and for thy truth: for thou hast magnified thy word above all thy name.

3 In the day when I cried thou answeredst me, *and* strengthenedst me *with* strength in my soul.

4 All the kings of the earth shall praise thee, O LORD, when they hear the words of thy mouth.

5 Yea, they shall sing in the ways of the LORD: for great *is* the glory of the LORD.

6 Though the LORD *be* high, yet hath he respect unto the lowly: but he proud he knoweth afar off.

7 Thou I walk in the midst of trouble, thou wilt revive me: thou shalt stretch forth thine hand against the wrath of mine enemies, and thy right hand shall save thee.

8 The LORD will perfect *that which* concerneth me: thy mercy, O LORD, *endureth* for ever: forsake not the works of thine own hands.

Psalm 139

To save a marriage.

To the chief musician, A Psalm of David.

O LORD, thou hast searched me, and known *me.*

2 Thou knowest my downsitting and mine uprising, thou understandest my thoughts afar off.

3 Thou compassest my path and my lying down, and art acquainted *with* all my ways.

4 For *there is* not a word in my tongue, but lo, O LORD, thou knowest it altogether.

5 Thou hast beset me behind and before, and laid thine hand upon me.

6 Such knowledge is too wonderful for me; it is high, I cannot *attain* unto it.

7 Whither shall I go from thy spirit? Or whither shall I flee from thy presence?

8 If I ascend up into heaven, thou *art* there: if I make my bed in hell, behold thou *art there.*

9 *If* I take the wings of the morning, and dwell in the uttermost parts of the sea;

10 Even there shall thy hand lead me, and thy right hand shall hold me.

11 If I say, Surely the darkness shall cover me; even the night shall be light about me.

12 Yea, the darkness hideth not from thee; but the night shineth as the day: the darkness and the light *are* both alike *to thee.*

13 For thou hast possessed my reins: thou hast covered me in my mother's womb.

14 I will praise thee; for I am fearfully and wonderfully made: marvelous *are* thy works; and *that* my soul knoweth right well.

15 My substance was not hid from thee, when I was made in secret, *and* curiously wrought in the lowest parts of the earth.

16 Thine eyes did see my substance, yet being unperfect; and in thy book all *my members* were written, *which* in continuance were fashioned, when *as yet there was* none of them.

17 How precious also are thy thoughts unto me, O God! How great is the sum of them!

18 If I should count them, they are more in number than the sand: when I awake, I am still with thee.

19 Surely thou wilt slay the wicked, O God: depart from me therefore, ye bloody men.

20 For they speak against thee wickedly, *and* thine enemies take *thy name* in vain.

21 Do not I hate them, O LORD, that hate thee? And am I not grieved with those that rise up against thee?

22 I hate them with perfect hatred: I count them mine enemies.

23 Search me, O God, and know my heart: try me, and know my thoughts:

24 And see if *there be any* wicked way in me, and lead me in the way everlasting.

Printed in Great Britain
by Amazon